Dinosaurs

D1326647

Scholastic Children's Books,
Euston House, 24 Eversholt Street,
London, NW1 1DB, UK

A division of Scholastic Ltd
London ~ New York ~ Toronto ~ Sydney ~ Auckland
Mexico City ~ New Delhi ~ Hong Kong

First published in the UK by Scholastic Ltd, 2018

Written by Jonathan Litton
Edited by Emily Ball
Illustrations Jon@KJA-artists.com
© Scholastic Children's Books, 2018

ISBN 978 1407 18907 9

Printed in China

2 4 6 8 10 9 7 5 3 1

Papers used by Scholastic Children's Books are made from wood
grown in sustainable forests.

www.scholastic.co.uk

CONTENTS

TERRIBLE LIZARDS

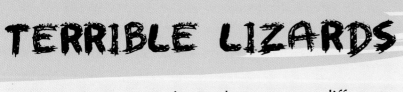

Millions of years ago, the Earth was a very different place. Gigantic creatures stomped through steamy swamps, swam through salty seas and soared through ancient skies. This was the age of the dinosaurs. Split into three periods – the Triassic (245 to 201 million years ago), the Jurassic (201 to 145 million years ago) and the Cretaceous (145 to 66 million years ago) – this age lasted nearly 180 million years.

The word dinosaur means 'terrible lizard' and many of these lizard-like beasts were truly terrifying carnivores (meat-eaters) like Tyrannosaurus rex. But others were harmless herbivores (plant-eaters) like Brontosaurus. While many were huge, there were also some miniature dinosaurs the size of present day chickens. From tiny Saltopus ('hopping foot') to mighty Argentinosaurus ('Argentinian lizard'), let's take a closer look at these terrible lizards…

DINOSAUR FAMILIES

Hundreds of dinosaur species have already been discovered and it's likely that hundreds more are waiting to be found. Many of the dinosaurs that have already been discovered belong to these main groups or families of related species:

Sauropods
(lizard-footed)

Growing up to 40 metres in length, these are the largest land animals the Earth has ever seen. These giant herbivores had to eat tonnes of leaves every day to stay so big.

Ceratopsians
(horned faces)

These herbivores had horns, spikes and frills on their faces – possibly for protection, but also probably for display and to help them attract a mate. Triceratops is the best known ceratopsian.

Lived in: the Cretaceous period

Lived in: the late Jurassic and early Cretaceous periods

Ankylosaurs (fused lizards)

With a full set of body armour, these were the armadillos of the prehistoric world. As well as bony plates, spikes and shields, they had club-like tails, which they used to beat off attackers.

Lived in: the late Jurassic and Cretaceous periods

Stegosaurs
(roof lizards)

These armoured dinosaurs used spikes and plates to defend themselves from attack or to attract mates. Modelling these spikes and plates here are Stegosaurus and Kentrosaurus.

Lived in: the late Jurassic and early Cretaceous periods

Theropods *(beast-footed)*

Theropods stood on two powerful legs and often had short arms. They ranged in length from 34 centimetres to 18 metres and included the mighty Tyrannosaurus rex and the quick-footed Velociraptor.

Lived in: the Triassic, Jurassic and Cretaceous periods

Ornithopods *(bird-footed)*

These medium and large herbivores had grinding teeth and cheek pouches, perfect for munching on plants. Included in this family is the iguana-like Iguanodon and the duck-billed Parasaurolophus, with its wonderful headcrest.

Lived in: the Triassic, Jurassic and Cretaceous periods

MIGHTY MEAT-EATERS

Some huge carnivorous (meat-eating) dinosaurs would have been feared by many other dinosaurs. With powerful jaws and claws, they could make a meal out of smaller, weaker creatures. Tyrannosaurus rex is the most famous, but he wasn't the only mighty meat-eater in town…

Saurophaganax *(lord of the lizard-eaters)*

Saurophaganax was the top predator of Jurassic North America. Diplodocus and Stegosaurus are thought to have been among its victims, and it probably ate the equivalent of 600 burgers every day.

Lived: late Jurassic
Found in: USA
Size: up to 13 metres long, weighing about 3,000 kilograms

Tyrannosaurus rex *(bully lizard king)*

T. rex chased after smaller dinosaurs at 30 kilometres per hour, then used his 30 centimetre-long teeth to rip their flesh apart. Or did he? Some scientists think the mighty 'bully lizard king' wasn't actually a very strong runner and mainly ate the remains of dinosaurs killed by other predators!

Lived: late Cretaceous
Found in: Canada, USA
Size: up to 12 metres long, weighing about 7,000 kilograms

Giganotosaurus *(giant southern lizard)*

Longer than T. rex, this giant lived millions of years earlier and may have hunted the massive sauropod, Argentinosaurus. Running at 50 kilometres per hour, you wouldn't want to get in the way of this colossal carnivore.

Lived: early Cretaceous
Found in: Argentina
Size: up to 14 metres long, weighing about 8,000 kilograms

Spinosaurus *(thorn lizard)*

Measuring as long as two buses from snout to tail, Spinosaurus is probably the longest land carnivore the Earth has ever seen, though T. rex and Giganotosaurus were heavier. Spinosaurus may have also been the first dinosaur that was able to swim.

Lived: late Cretaceous
Found in: Egypt, Morocco
Size: up to 18 metres long, weighing about 4,000 kilograms

DINOSAUR DEFENDERS

With so many mighty meat-eaters around, harmless herbivores (plant-eaters) needed to watch out. Some sported spikes, horns and armour to defend themselves against predators. Here are some of the best battle-dressed examples...

Stegosaurus *(roof lizard)*

Slowcoach 'Steg' is thought to have had a top speed of only 7 kilometres per hour, so it needed all of its spikes to defend itself from predators. It famously had a brain the size of a walnut.

Lived: late Jurassic
Found in: USA
Size: up to 9 metres long, weighing around 3,000 kilograms

Kentrosaurus *(sharp-pointed lizard)*

Despite being smaller than Stegosaurus, Kentrosaurus was like a Stegosaurus Plus. It had sharp spikes on its back and tail, and it could swing its whip-like tail at over 100 kilometres per hour at any prowling predators!

Lived: late Jurassic
Found in: Tanzania
Size: up to 5 metres long, weighing around 2,000 kilograms

Triceratops *(three-horned face)*

This three-horned beast weighed as much as two elephants and had three horns to fend off its enemies … particularly T. rex, which lived around the same time.

Lived: late Cretaceous
Found in: USA
Size: up to 9 metres long, weighing between 4,000 and 6,000 kilograms

Kosmoceratops *(decorative-horned face)*

Why stop at three horns? Kosmoceratops had as many as fifteen. The team who discovered this dinosaur in 2010 thought the horns were for show as well as defence.

Lived: late Cretaceous
Found in: USA
Size: about 4.5 metres long, weighing up to 2,000 kilograms

Ankylosaurus *(fused lizard)*

This tank-like dinosaur was covered from head to toe in amazing armour – even its eyelids had protection. It used its club-like tail to bash attackers. Its only weak point was its soft belly.

Lived: late Cretaceous
Found in: Canada, USA
Size: about 7 metres long, weighing between 4,000 and 7,000 kilograms

HUGE PLANT-EATERS

Some dinosaurs didn't use spikes, horns or armour to defend themselves from attack. Instead they used their size! Simply by being huge, other dinosaurs would mostly leave them alone. These gentle giants were herbivores (plant-eaters), and had to eat enormous quantities to feed their gigantic bodies.

Diplodocus (double beam)

This super slow plant-eating giant became famous when a nearly complete skeleton of one was found in 1898. This was special because normally scientists have to work out the size of dinosaurs from only a few bones. Since then, replicas of these bones have been displayed in museums all over the world.

Brachiosaurus (arm lizard)

Brachiosaurus ate up to 400 kilograms of plants every day, and its giraffe-like neck helped it to reach leaves as high as 12 metres off the ground.

Lived: late Jurassic
Found in: Algeria, Portugal, Tanzania, USA
Size: up to 30 metres long, weighing as much as 70,000 kilograms

Lived: late Jurassic
Found in: USA
Size: up to 30 metres long, weighing as much as 20,000 kilograms

Supersaurus *(super lizard)*

Super in name and super in size, this was a classic sauropod ('lizard foot'). The most famous specimen found is named Jimbo and he lives in a museum in Wyoming, USA.

Lived: early Cretaceous
Found in: USA
Size: about 35 to 40 metres long, weighing between 30,000 and 100,000 kilograms

Argentinosaurus
(Argentinian lizard)

Possibly the biggest dinosaur of all, Argentinosaurus might have weighed as much as a blue whale and took 40 years to grow to its massive adult size. Giganotosaurus is perhaps the only predator that could have toppled it, but only if a group of Giganotosauruses hunted in a pack.

Lived: late Cretaceous
Found in: Argentina
Size: about 35 metres long, weighing between 70,000 and 100,000 kilograms

9

MINIATURE MARVELS

In a land of giants, some tiny dinosaurs proved that mini could be mighty. Just as the sauropods used their huge size as a defence, tiny dinosaurs were often simply too small for big predators to bother with, so size helped to keep them alive, too!

Let's meet some of these miniature marvels…

Microraptor *(tiny robber)*

Weighing only a kilogram, and sporting feathers, Microraptor looked a bit like an early bird. Hundreds of fossils of Microraptor have been found around the world, meaning it was probably very common.

Lived: early Cretaceous   **Found in:** numerous locations, mainly China

Compsognathus *(pretty jaw)*

This turkey-sized dinosaur ate lizards and insects, so it had to be lightning quick to catch them. Speediness also meant it could avoid being eaten.

Lived: late Jurassic   **Found in:** France, Germany

Bambiraptor *(bambi robber)*

One of the best-named dinosaurs around, the first Bambiraptor skeleton was found in 1993 by Wes Linster, who was only 14 at the time! This tiny, agile creature is thought to have had some feathers, giving it a bird-like (rather than deer-like) appearance.

Lived: late Cretaceous   **Found in:** USA

Deinonychus *(terrible claw)*

At about 3 metres in length, 'terrible claw' was a giant among the smaller dinosaurs and may have used its sharp, spiky claws on the back of its feet to fend off any attackers.

Lived: early Cretaceous   **Found in:** USA

Saltopus *(hopping foot)*

Tiny Saltopus weighed only 1 kilogram and is thought to have been quick and agile, so it could catch insects.

Lived: late Triassic   **Found in:** UK

Shuvuuia *(bird)*

Fossils of this bird-like dinosaur were found in Mongolia. At 60 centimetres in length, it is one of the smallest known dinosaurs. When scientists saw its shape and structure, they named it after the Mongolian word for bird, *shuvuu*.

Lived: late Cretaceous   **Found in:** Mongolia

Big babies

Baby sauropods were tiny dinosaurs too, despite adults being bigger than double-decker buses. When sauropods hatched, they weighed about 5 kilograms, before growing 10,000 times heavier. This is one of the biggest transformations in any living thing ever seen on Earth.

WINGED WONDERS

While dinosaurs ruled the Earth, pterosaurs ('winged lizards') ruled the skies. These flying reptiles included the largest flying creatures the planet has ever seen, with some as large as a jet and as tall as a giraffe!

Let's meet some of the species that soared high up above, while the dinosaurs roared down below...

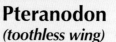

Pteranodon
(toothless wing)

Pteranodon is a classic pterosaur. Its wings didn't have feathers, but were made from skin which stretched out from a super-long finger!

Lived: late Cretaceous
Found in: USA
Size: nearly 2 metres tall, with a wingspan of up to 8 metres, weighing 22 kilograms

Dimorphodon *(two-shaped teeth)*

As its name suggests, Dimorphodon had two types of teeth, but scientists are not sure whether it used these to bite into fish or insects or both.

Lived: Jurassic
Found in: locations in Europe, USA
Size: about 0.6 metres long, with double the wingspan, weighing less than a kilogram

Tapejara *(the old being)*

Many pterosaurs had headcrests extending high above their heads, and the Tapejara's is among the biggest ever discovered. It was probably for display.

Quetzalcoatlus
(named after an Aztec god)

Quetzalcoatlus stood taller than a giraffe, and must have been the master of the ancient skies. It's hard to think that such a huge creature could have actually taken off.

Lived: late Cretaceous
Found in: USA
Size: about 5 to 6 metres long with a wingspan of over 10 metres, weighing about 90 to 115 kilograms

Lived: early Cretaceous
Found in: Brazil
Size: about 1.5 metres tall, with a wingspan of up to 3.5 metres, weighing around 35 to 40 kilograms

13

MONSTERS OF THE DEEP

The prehistoric oceans were full of super-sized monsters. Ancient sharks were twice as big as modern ones and plenty of fierce predators roamed the seas. Some of them were called plesiosaurs ('almost lizards') – they were not-quite dinosaurs, but shared many similarities.

Liopleurodon *(smooth-sided teeth)*

Liopleurodon is thought to be one of the most powerful carnivores of all time, with a strong bite that could rival T. rex. It was also a powerful swimmer, which came in handy as the ocean was full of hungry predators!

Lived: mid Jurassic
Size: between 6 to 10 metres long, weighing about 2,500 kilograms

Mosasaurus
(lizard of the Meuse River)

Mosasaurus could grow longer than T. rex and used its speed and sharp teeth to hunt prey. Similar to snakes, these creatures had jaws that could expand, allowing them to swallow large prey whole.

Lived: late Cretaceous
Size: about 15 metres long, weighing over 13,000 kilograms

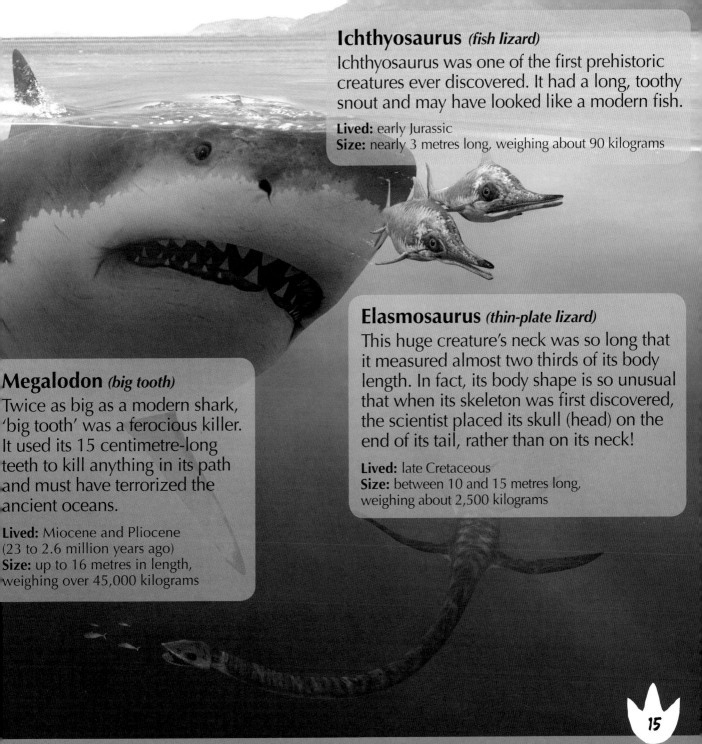

Ichthyosaurus *(fish lizard)*

Ichthyosaurus was one of the first prehistoric creatures ever discovered. It had a long, toothy snout and may have looked like a modern fish.

Lived: early Jurassic
Size: nearly 3 metres long, weighing about 90 kilograms

Megalodon *(big tooth)*

Twice as big as a modern shark, 'big tooth' was a ferocious killer. It used its 15 centimetre-long teeth to kill anything in its path and must have terrorized the ancient oceans.

Lived: Miocene and Pliocene (23 to 2.6 million years ago)
Size: up to 16 metres in length, weighing over 45,000 kilograms

Elasmosaurus *(thin-plate lizard)*

This huge creature's neck was so long that it measured almost two thirds of its body length. In fact, its body shape is so unusual that when its skeleton was first discovered, the scientist placed its skull (head) on the end of its tail, rather than on its neck!

Lived: late Cretaceous
Size: between 10 and 15 metres long, weighing about 2,500 kilograms

FOSSIL FINDS

How do we know so much about dinosaurs if they've been extinct for millions of years? Because of fossils. When some dinosaurs died in watery areas, their bodies quickly rotted away, leaving their bones.

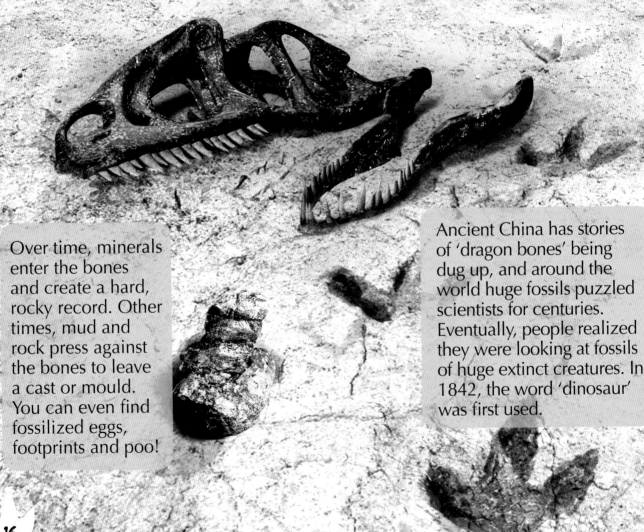

Over time, minerals enter the bones and create a hard, rocky record. Other times, mud and rock press against the bones to leave a cast or mould. You can even find fossilized eggs, footprints and poo!

Ancient China has stories of 'dragon bones' being dug up, and around the world huge fossils puzzled scientists for centuries. Eventually, people realized they were looking at fossils of huge extinct creatures. In 1842, the word 'dinosaur' was first used.

The Bone Wars

From 1877 to 1892, American palaeontologists (fossil hunters) Othniel Charles Marsh and Edward Drinker Cope had a huge rivalry. They both dug up hundreds of fossils and raced to name new dinosaurs. However, they also spied on each other, fought with each other and even used dynamite to stop the other … you can see why their rivalry has become known as the 'Bone Wars'! Both men eventually lost all their money because of their constant battling against one another, but between them they named over 130 new species of dinosaurs.

She Sells Seashells

Mary Anning was born in 1799 in Dorset, England. She used to walk along the beach with her dog collecting shells to sell to tourists. One day, she saw what looked like a skeleton sticking out of the rocks. It was a fossilized ichthyosaurus ('fish lizard'). After this she went on to find and sell many more fossils. Despite her lack of education, she also researched and wrote about the fossils she found in great detail. Although many people disregarded her work and she was never properly published, she eventually gained respect from scientists in London, who were amazed by her extraordinary fossils.

PREHISTORIC TIMELINE

Prehistory covers a long, long time – everything from billions of years ago to about 5,000 years ago. Dinosaurs lived from about 245 to 66 million years ago. But not all dinosaurs lived side by side. In fact, less time separates humans from T. rex than separates T. rex from Stegosaurus! Here's a handy timeline to help understand just how much has changed in all of this time.

Fascinating Fact

Dinosaurs roamed the Earth for less than 4% of the planet's history!

Cenozoic Era
(time of recent life)
66 million years ago to present

At the end of the Mesozoic Era, there was a mass extinction. About three-quarters of the animals and plants on Earth died out, including almost all the dinosaurs, pterosaurs and plesiosaurs.

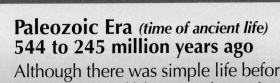

Paleozoic Era *(time of ancient life)*
544 to 245 million years ago

Although there was simple life before, this time period saw an explosion of life on Earth – it developed from single-celled organisms to complex plants and animals. The first trees, first insects, first four-legged animals and first reptiles emerged during this era. It was a time of dramatic change.

Mesozoic Era *(time of middle life)*
245 to 66 million years ago

Dinosaurs evolved during this time period and so too did plesiosaurs, pterosaurs, birds and mammals. The Mesozoic Era is subdivided into the Triassic period, which featured the first dinosaurs; the Jurassic period, featuring Brachiosaurus and the first Stegosaurus; and the Cretaceous period featuring Spinosaurus, T. rex and Triceratops.

Mammals became dominant, which is why the Cenozoic Era is sometimes called the 'Age of the Mammals'. Humans only evolved very, very recently (just a few million years ago) – a blink of an eye in geological time!

19

EXTINCTION EVENT

Around 66 million years ago, most dinosaurs around the world became extinct. Scientists are still puzzled as to why this happened, but their leading theories are explained below...

Asteroid impact

Could a large asteroid have hit the Earth and killed off the dinosaurs? A big enough impact would create dust and would block out sunlight, killing off many plants and animals around the globe. This theory is the most widely accepted.

Climate change

Could an ice age or other big change in the climate have killed off the dinosaurs? Some scientists think so, however there isn't much evidence to suggest an ice age occurred at the time of the extinction.

Competition from mammals

The fossil record shows that many small mammals survived the extinction event. Could these animals have feasted on dinosaur eggs or the plants that dinosaurs would normally have eaten, until the dinosaurs died out?

Volcanic eruption

Or could a gigantic volcanic eruption have caused the death of the dinosaurs? There's less evidence for this than the asteroid theory, but some people still argue it is the best explanation.

Dinosaurs live on!

It's still a mystery why dinosaurs died out yet other species such as crocodiles lived on. However, even though dinosaurs themselves died out, today there are over 10,000 species of living dinosaurs, better known as birds. As strange as it sounds, modern birds evolved from theropod dinosaurs, like T. rex and Velociraptor.

DINOSAUR DICTIONARY

asteroid – a rock from space; sometimes asteroids hit the Earth

carnivore – meat-eater

Cretaceous period – last period of time when the dinosaurs lived, about 145 to 66 million years ago

dinosaur – lizard-like creatures which lived on Earth millions of years ago; name means 'terrible lizard'

era – a period of time, which is significantly different from the surrounding time periods

eruption – an explosion of a volcano

extinct – died out; a species is extinct if it has no living individuals left

fossil – evidence of an animal, plant, footprint, poo or similar preserved in rock

headcrest – a feature sticking up from the head of some dinosaurs and pterosaurs

herbivore – plant-eater

Jurassic period – middle period of time when the dinosaurs lived, about 201 to 145 million years ago

mammal – the dominant type of animal of the current era; warm-blooded with a backbone, gives milk to its young and usually gives birth to live young

pack – group of animals; also known as a herd

palaeontologist – a scientist that studies fossilized animals and plants

period – a division of time, shorter than an era. For example, the Mesozoic Era is divided into three periods: the Triassic period, the Jurassic period and the Cretaceous period

plesiosaur – a group of prehistoric sea creatures related to dinosaurs meaning 'almost lizards'. Not all prehistoric sea creatures were plesiosaurs

predator – a carnivorous animal which hunts other animals for food

prehistory – any time before recorded history, so any time before about 5,000 years ago

pterosaur – prehistoric flying creatures that were related to dinosaurs; the name means 'winged lizards'

species – a 'type' of living thing different from all other types; humans, pandas, Tyrannosaurus rexes and Brontosauruses are all different species

theory – an explanation for why things happened, but an explanation which has not yet been 100% confirmed; for example, there are several theories why the dinosaurs became extinct

Triassic period – first period of time when the dinosaurs lived, about 245 to 201 million years ago